2012 TO ONENESS

WHAT WORLD DO YOU CHOOSE?

Within each of us there lies a deep passion that we are born with. Over the years we either tap into that passion or let it die. As I read Lizette's poems it gives me hope that as we age with wisdom, we can tap into that passion and allow it to become our reality. That's what these poems say to me.

—Charlie Johansen-Adams
Leading Edge Consulting

I can't say enough about how your poems have touched my soul. Your poems hit the sweet spot in me that identifies with your profound expressions of feelings and experiences. You always uplift and provide me with "aha" moments. Sharing your insights with others has been tremendously meaningful to me. I love your work. PLEASE don't ever stop!

—Louanne Persons, Artist

They met, two old friends, in beautiful Ventana Canyon. One of them heartsick from the senseless death of her seventeen-year-old-grandson and soul weary from years of dysfunctional relationships, and the other newly in touch with her Source-driven ability to create poetry. They spent that long weekend talking, meditating, and hiking the desert terrain pushing one another to go further, dig deeper, and truly see life as it is meant to be lived. And the poetry poured over both of them giving healing, inspiration and promises for the future. Thank you, Lizette, for the gift of your poetry, which continues to center me as I walk my path with a lighter step

—Pam Walling, Teacher

Spiritual expansion begins with the exploration of our emotional reaction to the great adventure called life. Lizette's poetry expresses her journey with an open heart, and with great courage she bares her soul.

—Len Whitebear, Sculptor

I am a big fan of Lizette's poetry. She has a way of writing that connects both the heart and the head, and leaves you a better person for the experience.

—Molly Merritt-Duren
Career Guidance Counselor

Lizette Stiehr has created in these poems words of comfort and struggle. They are expressions of the unique balance between Nature, Spirit, and the God of Unity. Thank you for sharing your beautiful gift with the world.

—Beverly A. Knox
Chief Financial Officer
FOCUS, Inc

Lizette's poetry amazingly, sensitively, and astutely transforms emotions, visuals and nature into the most fabulous flow of energy in the form of sound, of words. Each poem is more beautiful than the one before.

—Jackie Van Dusen
Light Sound Therapy

Thank you, Lizette, for sharing your clear and awakened poetry. To be pointed in a direction where truth can be recognized, rather than told what is, is so much more powerful in assisting people with their shift.

—Katie Wood, Grant Writer

In the coming year of 2012, Lizette's poems will transmit the light to God's Will and Oneness with you. One stanza in her poem, "The Great Will," is:

"I am the will of God"
does not make me God,
but it clears God
to full rights to me.

Each and every stanza of Lizette's poems brings God's Inhale of light. After each stanza you will come to realize the Oneness you have with God and self. Read her poems and feel her expressions of love of self and humanity.

—Stanley Sears
Global Positioning Services

2012 TO ONENESS

WHAT WORLD DO YOU CHOOSE?

LIZETTE ESTELLE STIEHR

NORTHBOOKS

Eagle River, Alaska

Interior Photos:

Pam Taylor, Sedona, Arizona

Todd Rector, Palmer, Alaska

Cover photo:

Dewitt Jones

Light in the Redwoods, #66, www.celebratewhatsright.com

Original Paintings and Sculpture shown in photographs:

Sarah Nano, Sedona, Arizona (paintings)

Star York, Santa Fe, New Mexico (sculpture)

Published by:

ႶORCႹBOOKS

11915 Lazy Street, Ste. C

Eagle River, Alaska 99577-7898

www.northbooks.com

Printed in the United States of America

ISBN 978-0-9830764-1-4

Library of Congress Control Number: 2011937564

DEDICATION

This book is dedicated to YOU, fellow traveler on this journey as we anchor increasing amounts of light and love, joy and peace into our precious human bodies and daily lives. I am so grateful to be sharing this path, this mission with you.

"In Lak'ech," I am another yourself.

MAY THE LESSONS BE GENTLE
AND THE JOY BE GREAT.

CONTENTS

FOREWORD

In this series of heartfelt poems, Lizette leads us through the portal of self-discovery and connection to Spirit, stories of light and darkness taking shape over time, millennia really, challenging each of us to question how we unconsciously (or not) respond to people and events in our lives. And how, on a greater scale, the raw energy of light and darkness culminates to serve or upset our world at large. We are called to love.

Lizette has the gift of opening ourselves to ourselves, examining how we can skillfully create love and balance through conscious awareness, day by day, moment by moment. Acknowledging fear, insecurity, cloudy emotions, and limitations, she gently trails us back to the question, now what? How do I move forward through these challenges with an open heart, and bigger yet, how can we collectively carry a greater vision of peace, clarity and right relationship?

Simply by sharing the light within us, the cupful of luminosity that at times, is shaded by dark clouds of confusion and turmoil. We must consciously water the tiny mustard seed of hope within our hearts with great vigilance, a task that is not as simple as it sounds. It requires prayer, awareness, a lifetime of practice, and still more prayer. We are called to love.

These poems celebrate and honor the beauty of oneness attained on this path of awareness and self-discovery. They are less of a "how to" approach, and more a "walk through" experience with Lizette at the helm. Through years of self-examination and watchful study of the dark and light forces in our lives, her personhood emanates an openness and curiosity she is eager to share.

I see Lizette as a wrangler, grounded in the earth, yet roping the sun, the stars and the moon, gathering the light by calling in joyful energy. She meets every gaze with a generous smile, and frankly, when I'm in her presence, I feel good.

And there is no better barometer of love than that.

—Monica Devine
Eagle River, Alaska
June, 2011

ACKNOWLEDGMENTS

Without Len Whitebear, I would not have become the person I am today. Her mother-bear love coupled with deep and ever-honest feedback, when I've been wise enough to ask for it, have guided me through thick and thin. Calling her my best friend is an understatement of the profound spiritual sisterhood that we have shared.

I so appreciate the many friends, co-workers, and blog strangers who have read my poetry and said such generous, kind and encouraging words about how the poems made them feel or think.

The true credit for the glorious outpouring of poetry from my soul found in this volume goes to my eleven higher selves that consciously and willingly started joining with me three decades ago. It is our merging of information, feelings and processing, joy and light that you experience in this book. Thank you: Uluteria, Eckaka, Laganat/Sanat, Chereen, Namu and the Hermit/Lantern plus the five beings from across the void. It is as we have jointly "scrubbed the pot," "cleaned off the glass" and "peeled the onion" to align our will(s) with the greater will that the voice and experiences of both processing and Oneness were recorded onto these pages. And, of course, the greatest gratitude is for the Creator of this amazing show.

A big thank you is due my publishers, Ray and Jan Holmsen, for their patience, humor and editing, ever supporting my voice.

And a most special thank you to my photojournalist cousin Pam Taylor and good friend and healer Todd Rector for allowing me to use their beautiful photos to feed your eyes as the words feed your mind and heart.

It is my deepest hope that the photos and word images together will feed your soul.

PREFACE

Our greatest mission, our true mission, is to bring light into the darkness. As adventurers, we have taken on form and walked away from the light of Oneness with Creator into the zone of free will where we have experimented deeply with the dark. In walking into free will, away from the light of Source, we have created a world where the light/dark balance is the equivalent of three cups of darkness compared to small dropper full of light. Imagine how thinly those limited light particles have been spread out. Now, 2012 has become one symbol of our about-face, our turning and beginning a march in the opposite direction toward Creator, towards Oneness with the light. While that may be difficult to see in the world reported upon by newspapers and TV news, that is because the dark sees the advancing light and is having to work overtime to maintain the same level of fear that has restricted us for millennium.

The poems in this volume record my journey of the last few years incorporating light into my life. They have poured themselves onto paper out of my soul's deepest longing for a way to express itself and our journey in this wondrous and difficult world.

The poems are divided into three sections, matching the title of the book. The first section, "2012," includes both what I have studied, "seen" through my guidance and experienced viscerally concerning 2012. The center section of the book, "to," are those poems that show my human struggles of walking the most light that I am capable of in both physical body and daily life. The third and last section of the book, "Oneness," are the poems written when my heart was wide open, truly feeling at one with all that is. Experiencing first hand "In Lak'ech," I am another yourself.

Those of us who have studied the Mayan calendar find it difficult to follow the format in which 2012 is publicized with such glamour and horror as the end of the world. It no more means the end of our world than the "end of the day" means there will be no more days. It means this cycle, this "day," is giving way to a new way, a new cycle, a new direction. It is a change, a shift, an ending of the old. And a significant one for Tera, our blessed planet as represented by the change we see in weather patterns as well as for the consciousness of humanity.

The Mayan calendar has been a significant part of my life. Since 1993 I have followed the sign of each day or day glyph. The Mayan calendar has several cycles which interface. Each of the twenty days in a unial (you can think of it as a sort of month) is assigned a day sign or glyph. You can think of each glyph as a metaphorical image (or carved figure) that carries a large amount of cosmic information around one theme. For example, the first glyph is Imix, primal nurturing. Additionally the calendar operates like gear wheels with the day sign or glyph interfacing with a thirteen-day count. So each day is assigned a number that combines with the glyph of the day to influence it. In addition to meditating on the glyph and number combinations each morning, I frequently find events during my day to reflect that energy.

On a larger scale the consciousness pioneers who have done the deep research on the Mayan calendar identify 2012 as an astronomy event. At winter solstice, December 21, our sun will align with the Great Central Sun in the center of our galaxy. Our familiar solar system, orbiting our local sun, orbits as a whole around Alcyon. Alcyon is the center sun of the seven sisters of the Pleiadian system. One of those seven sisters is named Maya. Our sun is the eighth sister. The Earth/Sun/Pleiadian cycle is at the end of a 26,000-year cycle. The entire Pleiadian system, including this solar ring, is at the end of a 230,000,000-year orbit around the Galactic Center. And the entire galaxy is at the completion of an infinitely larger orbit around the Great Central Sun. All three cycles are synchronistically finishing the last steps of a spiral dance making this a major transition time.

All of the changes that we see in our world and feel internally as we approach 2012 speak to the transformation that is taking place. It shows in our lives as a shift in the balance between the light and the dark. And the shift is happening not only here on Earth, but throughout our solar system and the galaxy. As humans on the planet Earth we continue to reside in a free-will zone, with our internal guidance (angels, guides) encouraging us moment by moment, if we are asking, to join in the up shifting of energies available now to all. The quarantine placed around the Earth many millennia ago has now been lifted.

My favorite "picture" or understanding of 2012 is that Creator breathes in and out over geological time. On the out-breath, consciousness travels far into the darkness, moving away from light and love, to explore the full parameters of free will. We humans came as brave explorers to try on this "free-will" zone, moving away from alignment with the divine will. We marched into the third dimension, spreading the light as thinly as was possible to maintain physical forms. We experimented with the dark, all the while closing down or denying the love and light that is the truth at our core.

That experiment is at an end now. In the greatest cycle 2012 represents the Earth's moving into the in-breath of Creator. Humanity is now supported in moving back into the light, into will alignment with Creator. Will alignment, chosen through our free will, brings us back into oneness. As we move into the light we take all of our experiences and growth with us. As we recognize the truth of ourselves, we expand to incorporate our merged selves and become a conscious member of our clan once again. Our "molecules" of awareness, while spreading ever farther apart, always respond to our harmonic signature song.

A return to Oneness no more means an eradiation of the self, an end to us, than 2012 means the end of our world.

—Lizette Stiehr
Eagle River, Alaska
September 23, 2011

Photo by Pam Taylor
Art by Sarah Nano

2012

To

Oneness

Reservations for 2012

Once the Cumberland Gap
was a "new pass."
Later Lewis and Clark explored
what the fifth dimension
native people lived,
but was "unexplored."
The gold miners
flooded the Chilkoot Trail
in the "Last Frontier."

Now we study and pack,
and make reservations
for our 2012 journey.

What world are we marching to,
reserving space in?
How much love,
how much kindness,
how much compassion,
how much peace and harmony
does it hold?
How much is in your life today?

The ratio in 2012
will be what you can hold,
will be what you choose.

And your choices
are reflected in
where your heart and head
spend their energy today.

What do you choose?

Photo by Pam Taylor

2012: The End? [1]

Is 2012 the end of our world?
No more than the
"end of the day"
means no more days.

A new era?
Oh yes.
A new day will dawn
on December 22, 2012,
the day after solstice.

Our clocks, our computers,
our thoughts and our lives
will roll over to the next
dawn.

And the thinning veils,
the increased light
in the light/dark balance
will guarantee
a new age.

No end of the world this,
but a beginning
of a better one.

Photo by Pam Taylor

2012 Creator's Breath[2]

As Creator EXHALED
we traveled deeply
into the darkness,
exploring our free will.

All the while
feeling abandoned
by Spirit.
When in truth
it was us
abandoning the
love of Creator.

On Creator's INHALE
we move into will alignment
with Creator/God/Source.

We move into love of self.
We discover and allow again
our love of both Source and self.

And we remember
that Creator is
within us.
That we are
ONE.

The Fall to 2012

Our souls came,
full of excitement,
as part of the
scientific experiment
of the FALL.

We came to spread the light
as far and wide and thinly
as possible.

Our clans faded out of view
as we marched deep
into the third dimension.
Entering deep into form,
into physical bodies.

We paraded into the dark
which appeared to grow.
It weighed upon us.
The light spread so thinly,
was a mere twelve drops of light
to three full cups of darkness.

Alone we appeared.
Alone we've felt,
wandering in the desert,
seeking water,
the light of our own truth.

Finally 2012 brings
that experiment to an end.

We can again see
through our merged selves
the clans that ever held us close.

The light is thickening.
The light is rebalancing
with the dark
at this glorious
"inhale" of Creator.

And we are reuniting
with ourselves, our clans,
and the Creator within,
back into
the One Light.

Photo by Pam Taylor

Photo by Todd Rector

Avalanche

No one snowflake
thinks it is responsible
for the avalanche.

Yet as each crystalline form
seeks to reflect the light,
the light switch
is turned on.

No more shoveling
out the dark.

The balance has shifted.
An avalanche of Light!

Photo by Pam Taylor
Painting by Sarah Nano

Kairos

In Greek
kairos is the point
where the shuttle
passes between warp and woof.
From the above to the below.

2012 is like
kairos.
We pass
from old his-story,
stuttering over fear
and control,
through the loosely woven fabric
to love and light.

Maybe this is how
it happens.
Those who choose
no change,
get to stay in his-story.

While those of us
busy diving
through the kairos point,
though the tapestry
weaving anew,
shift dimensions.

Or is it we're all
kairosing,
weaving the tapestry
of our choice?

2012 and James Bond[3]

Arjuna Ardagh,
I so love your image
of 2012 as the end
of a James Bond movie.

The forces of evil,
ever clandestine and international,
appear benevolent while
attempting world control.

All aligned
against one individual.
One suave, fearless
James Bond, filled with
life, humor and lust,
who is living in the moment.

In a nail-biter to the end,
Bond discovers and takes on,
the robotic forces of evil
unraveling their plan.

And here we are as humanity.
With one percent of us funny humans
holding forty percent of the world's wealth.
Transparency now unveiling
the greed over integrity
at the core of our old system.

The translucents are those
who have touched
the Oneness.

Those who have
walked through the illusion
of "he who dies
with the most toys, wins."
Those whose minds
no longer master them,
but rather their hearts.
Those who know the truth
that we are all related.
Those who have experienced
we are just one molecule
of the Greater Body
of the Creator.

The translucents are poised,
suave and fearless,
humorously getting the
great comic joke,
and living in the moment.

The translucents,
in a nail-biter to the end,
are no longer living in fear.
They are no longer
falling for the buy-more,
spend-more,
have-more "solution."

Instead they are creating
their own lives
of love and joy
with peace at the center.
Turning evil on its
pointy little head,
and living life forward.

Photo by Todd Rector

Time Leapt Forward

Time leapt forward
last night.
We lost the hour
granted us last fall.

We sacrifice that hour
to lengthening days
and hints of spring.
There's water on the road.
Snow is dirty and disappearing,
tree branches naked,
and mountain shoulders'
baring brown ridges
through the white.

In Alaska we know
spring sleeps yet,
buds a full month away
. . . at least.

Yet our soul,
our spirit,
stirs out of winter's doldrums,
shivering in anticipation.
The lost hour,
 a small price to pay.

Much like 2012 coming.
You can feel the shimmer
of the "spring" coming,
but there's not much evidence yet.

Labor & Delivery

When my mother labored
and I was delivered,
daddies and husbands
were not allowed near.

Moms, flat on their backs,
were not present but drugged.
Babies arrived asleep,
"under the influence."

One generation later
when I had my babies,
moving around encouraged,
midwives working with doctors.
Pain meds available
but not pushed, nor taken.

Baby's daddy and
mother's friends were
present and involved.
Babies were once again,
delivered to wide-awake love.

Now each of us is
birthing our post-2012 world,
deep in those labor pains.

The world is not going away
in 2012.
But right now, you
are determining what
that new world

will be like for you.
Are you laboring,
flat on your back,
listening to instructions
from someone else?

Are you accepting the anesthesia
that the economic powers
offer you minute by minute?
Another credit card application.
And you're already approved!!
Buy more. Have more.
Show off more, but don't think.

Or are you in labor,
breathing with the pain
and grateful for each respite?
Are you lining your bedside
with friends and family and guides
who truly support you?

Are you using
meditation,
a walk in the sun,
a funny movie,
coffee with a friend
for your pain meds?

We are all laboring.
And we will deliver.

I want my new life
to be delivered to
wide-awake love and joy,
and deep peace.

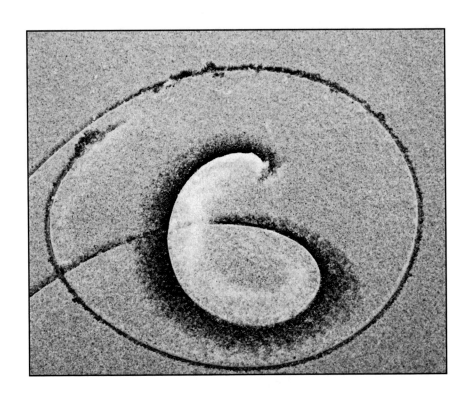

Photo by Todd Rector

The Chalice and the Blade[4]

Our souls marched
deep into this third dimension,
spreading the light thinly.
We carried our swords,
our masculine blades,
to carve the dense fear
into bite-sized pieces.
We've carried that blade
as our protection, our power,
for millennium.

And now
we march back out
to a world where the dark
is just stripes between the light.

We lay down our swords,
our blades of the third dimension,
and accept the chalice
of the fifth dimension.

To accept the chalice,
is to accept that we are at
at the peak of the third dimension
represented by a pyramid pointing up, a blade.

Now we are readying
for entry into the
inverted pyramid from above
representing female energy.
The overlay of the two creates
the chalice of the fifth dimension.

A dimension of balance
requiring each of us to acknowledge
ourselves as co-creators of our reality,
through collaboration and cooperation
between male and female energy
acknowledging the unity of being one with all.

We turn our back on fear
and face the light
that radiates from within us.
We march in the direction of change.

It is a new day,
a new year,
and a very different millennium.

If we choose that.

Photo by Pam Taylor

The Great Will[5]

"Not my will, but Thy will"
is a lie.
It separates what is one.

"I am willing to will the will of God"
was me ever reaching
closer to the truth
that we are ONE.

"I am willing the will of God"
was reaching closer yet,
toes in the water of truth,
ankles in the water of the Beloved.

"I am the will of God"
is my truth.
The angels speak
when I'm headed awry.

I am committed
to the path, ever inward,
ever bigger.
And always finding
the shadow places
that need a bit more light,
or lots more light
in the ocean of love
within.

"I am the will of God"
does not make me God,
but it clears God

to full rights to me.

"I am the will of God"
makes me an atom of Her toenail,
and fills every cell of me
with the Beloved.

"I am the will of God."
Help me find, daily,
the patterns in me
that aren't yet love.

Made to Be Unfolded, Not Molded[6]

We children of the light
are made to be unfolded.
We're not made to be molded.
Yet we have allowed ourselves
to be molded by fear,
by the shoulds and ought tos
and gotta haves.

And all the while we crave
the unfolding of our hearts
to open new and bigger spaces
from which to love.
To love others and even better,
to love ourselves.

And all the while we crave
our hearts unfolding into peace.
Unfolding to claim those choices
that help us find and live in peace.
The peace within us,
the only peace we can choose.

And all the while we crave
unfolding into joy
in the simplest of ways.
Turning our face,
to follow the light
just like the sunflower
following the sun.
Turning our head
into the wind
allowing our hair to wave

joy to the world.
May we all
unfold our now moment
to embrace
love
and joy
and peace.

Photo by Pam Taylor

Photo by Pam Taylor

Paradox of the Cornucopia[7]

The Holy Grail of self
when emptied,
when poured out
in meditation,
fills from the
wellspring within.

The paradox of
"the cornucopia,
of emptiness and harvest,
the still place that
lies open and fallow"
is solved.

From within the cornucopia
wells up the deep abiding love
that flows from and for self,
from and for the
Creatoress within.

And joy wells up,
the joy of contentment
and excitement combined.

And peace wells up
that allows acceptance
of all that is.

The cornucopia is "empty,"
and we are harvesting
a thickening of the light.

Photo by Pam Taylor

You Choose[8]

A mother stands,
pudgy fingers
framing her face.
"ook at me, Mama,
ook at me."
Full attention demanded.

Christ stands,
arms outstretched.
Each of us choosing
how much of his attention
we think we deserve.

The Creator stands,
arms behind Her back.
A humble servant,
loyal to our peace and joy,
and equally loyal to our
judgement and fear.
Moving only to create
upon our request.

What do YOU choose?

Poem previously published in the *Sedona Journal*,
October, 2010.

Photo by Todd Rector

2012

To

Oneness

Photo by Pam Taylor

Ground Hog Day[9]

Imbolc or
midwinter.
Groundhog Day
by another name.
Marmot Day in Alaska.
I watch Bill Murray
fall in love with Andy McDowell
again and again and again.

Awaking to yesterday
morning for 365 days.
What do you do with
yesterday over and over?

You wail and moan.
You beg for help.
You rage and rob a bank.
You resign and try suicide
repeatedly and unsuccessfully.
You learn to play the piano.
You learn how good it
feels to help others.
You fall in love with inner beauty.
You try to make her/him love you.
You finally learn to let go,
and love comes to you,
and life moves on.

Photo by Pam Taylor
Painting by Sarah Nano

Shift Happens[10]

I shift from
goals for just me,
to goals for my children.
I am a mother now.
Shift Happens!

I shift from
working for the state,
to working for my soul.
I am growing.
Shift happens!

I shift from
a workaholic life
to a sailing-away life.
I try on the party dress.
Shift Happens!

I shift from
being the healer,
to being healed.
I glow.
Shift Happens!

Today I shift
from being loved
for my accomplishments,
to being loved for me.
Shift Happens!

Today I shift from
loving you for
what you've done,
to loving you
for being you.
Shift Does Happen!

Photo by Pam Taylor

The Path[11]

I arrived at Coeur D'Alene,
the campground above Hope, Alaska,
in the sunshine
at the end of August.

I prepare to walk
the familiar short path
through deep trees
towards the hills.

The bridge, where
we played billy goats gruff
with the children,
is exactly the same.

The devil's club
and ferns sparkle
with raindrops.

But the path,
where I've come for
the fall colors
on my birthday
year after year,
is totally different.

Spruce beetle kill
has downed the big pines,
blocking the path,
routing one far uphill.

Now light floods into
what was once
deep forest with a single
pine-needled trail.

It is so odd
to have more light,
yet the path is not passable.

How like my inner life:
flooded with light,
sparkling with reflected
water drops of all colors.
The sky is huge.
I can see the mountains.
on three sides of me.
But the old familiar trail
is impassible.

The old path is gone
of service to others,
regardless of the cost to me.
The old path of giving when
I've no more to give
has become impassable.

Now the path is
rerouted anew,
unknown,
unclear.
And yet
I serve the light.

I serve the light
created by my intention,

defined from within,
not from without.
The old martyr
definition of service
no longer works.
There is no victim
here within me.

I serve the light
of peace and contentment,
of joy and harmony
and growth.

The growth of finding
the new path
that releases me
from the old patterns.

The old patterns of
"A good woman gives more
than she has,"
"A good woman stays
until death,"
"A good woman
never gets angry."

This weekend
I camp alone.
Filling my cup
with the silence of
the creek's running,
the raven's call and
the tide surging in and out.

I could have stayed
to help with the grandchildren.
A "good woman" would have.
I've graduated.

I graduate to a path
that unfolds right
in front of me.

I graduate to knowing
I have to fill my own well
in order to walk with Tera.

I graduate to a path
of incredible beauty.
My eyes drink all the hues
of green before me,
from the neon yellow green
of the devil's club to
the black green of the spruce
stands on the mountainside.

My eyes drool before the
tide's reflection of the blue sky
combined with the milky-grey silt
creating silver-grey shadowed water.

I graduate into
loving me enough
to fill my well
with the intention of joy and peace.

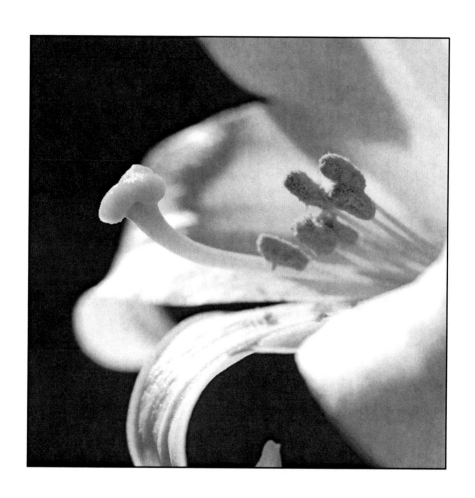

Photo by Pam Taylor

Deliver Us[12]

"Deliver Us!"
sing the Hebrews,
under pharaoh.
Save us.
You do it.

Come, my white knight
in shining armor,
save me.
You do it.

Come back, Messiah,
come deliver us
from the darkness
we've created.
Carry us to the light.
You do it.

Suddenly I hear
in the call,
"Everybody wants
a ride to heaven,
but nobody wants
to make the climb."
You carry me.
You do it.

Suddenly I hear
the recognition
in the call,
of me being
the victim.

You save me.
You do it.

How can I
ask for that?
I believe
"It is no longer
the time of
great spiritual leaders.
It is now the time
of great spirits, instead."

I am the only one
who can deliver me
from my fears,
my self-imposed
limitations.

It is time to claim
the wings of my light
and fly in lightness
and humor,
into the accountability
of being fully
responsible for my life

It is time to break the bonds
of my inner wars,
my fears of ridicule,
my wanting so
to have a community
of like-minded great spirits

I carry me.
I do it.

Photo by Pam Taylor

I Scrub the Pot 2 [13]

I dedicated this lifetime
to scrubbing the pot.

I came in with
so much energy
and so much residue.

I could always walk outside,
"run for no reason,"
or stand in my mulberry tree
to pour out the "old" water.

And each night
the pot/chalice/grail
would refill with clean new water
of the truth of my being.

But during each day
I'd find new places
to scrub the pot.
The places of judgment
toward myself and others
that my Virgo nature
was so good at identifying,
and the water would blacken.

Now it's meditation
that empties the pot,
that clears the water.
There is less residue each year.
Yet the process
repeats itself.

Photo by Pam Taylor

Paper Dolls

I so remember my paper dolls.
Cardboard figures
upon which I
could fold the
fancy dresses
I dreamed
of wearing.

My soul is like
that cardboard doll.
Folding life's characteristics:
jeans and car keys of mom,
the suit/uniform of work,
the snowsuit of play
to cover the naked light.

The Mission[14]

The mission,
our mission,
my mission
is to bring light
into the darkness.

My mission is
to bring
my light
to this reality.

It is my mission
to light
the space
that I inhabit.

It's NOT my mission
to bring my light
into the darkness
of another.

It's NOT my mission
to save anyone else
from their reality.

It's NOT my job
to make sure
others do a level of
the light/dark balance
that is comfortable
for me.

We each are masters.
We each get to select
the balance of
the light and dark
that we carry
in our lives.

Just as I get to select
the balance that works
for me.

I honor your path.
I honor my path.

Photo by Todd Rector

I Have No Authority Figure[15]

My Virgo-ness so loves
order, outlines and org charts.

But I no longer recognize
any external authority figure.

There is no God out there,
only a huge Creator in here,

with whom
I AM ONE.

Photo by Pam Taylor

Marrying Your Dark Side[16]

I always thought
my internal "marriage"
would look like balancing the
male and female energy within.

Now I see
it's the discovering,
the allowing
of my dark side
into an acceptance
of Oneness within me.

The original discovery is
fraught with
denial and withholding,
attempts to eradicate.

The original discovery is
made with tears,
recriminations and
self judgment.

All moving toward
the oasis of allowing,
of accepting.

Accepting that my
ego, my personality
is a gift from Source
that individuates me.
I am one.

Photo by Pam Taylor

E-Motion[17]

Emotion
is energy
in motion.
E-motion.

I find and feel
the energy,
the frequency
of my insecurity.

I forgive
the part of me,
that so wishes
I'd do it better,
hold more strongly.

I want to hold strong,
yet my Virgo mutable self
is dedicated to dissolving
and transforming.

True transformation
comes through forgiveness.
I allow forgiveness.
I forgive me.

The Road Less Traveled[18]

The road forks
in front of us,
moment by moment.
Choice in the split second
between thought
and words or action.

Do I choose
the old,
the familiar?

Or do I choose
to say my inconvenient truth,
not valued or appreciated?

I choose the fork
so at odds with
my mother's pattern:
it has to look good
to others.

I choose
my center of gravity.
"No I'm not the one
to do that."

Then I find myself
feeling others
are upset with me
for my new boundaries.
Yet, when I ask,
no one is upset

but me.
It's all my projection.

With new paths,
it's so expensive
not to take them.

It's so costly
to continue on the
the old paths of
having to look good
on the surface,
while half-baked inside.

I stand
tall and true
in my truth
as I take the
fork of light,
the road less traveled.

Photo by Pam Taylor
Painting by Sarah Nano

60

The Roadrunner[19]

The roadrunner
assumes the plank position:
head forward, tail flat out
to scuttle across the yard.

He is comical
in his intense hurry
to arrive . . . where?

As we scuttle,
at 75 miles an hour
in our hard-shelled carapaces,
we are hurrying
 to arrive . . . where?

Working in Our Sleep[20]

It is at work
that we are asleep.
At work on the
never-ending "to do" list.
Work harder.
Work more.
No time for play.
We are working in our sleep.

For it is in play,
in joy and laughter
that we awaken,
that we en-light-en.
It is as we play
that our hearts open
to others and with others.

Narada, the great saint,
acted as a postman
between heaven and earth.

An ancient sage, meditating
and fasting endlessly,
asked Narada how long
until I'm enlightened?

A young man was
under the same tree,
playing music and dancing.

In heaven Narada asks
timelines for both

and returns to the tree.
The sage is bitterly angry
hearing he has three more
lifetimes to enlightenment.

Narada tells the dancing man
he has as many lifetimes as
leaves on the tree.
The young man laughs,
"Only as many
leaves as on this tree?
Easy. Think of all
the trees on the planet,
and for me, only the leaves
of this one."

And in that instant,
he was enlightened.

It is as we work
that we are asleep.
It is as we play
that we awaken,
that we en-light-en.

Photo by Pam Taylor

Slow Down

As life speeds up,
the sanest response
is to slow down.
Emulate the praying mantis.

Bring the outside inside.
Feeling deep gratitude,
absorbing the beauty of
abstract bare-branch lines
against a grey sky with
snow piled and clumped
on every line.
Stark beauty
that turns you inward
to gratitude.

Photo by Todd Rector

In-Form-Mation[21]

When information
comes in
and I choose to accept it,
it becomes my reality.

He said,
she offered,
they announced.

Other's reality
comes in as in-form-mation.
It walks "in formation."
If I choose to accept it,
it then takes "form"
as my reality.

The reality I choose is:
May the lessons be gentle
and the joy be great.

Photo by Pam Taylor

Praying Mantis[22]

The praying mantis
perches in stillness,
forelegs in prayer position,
absorbing the healing
of the green surrounding him.

He prays that we too,
collective humanity,
can perch or kneel in stillness
and absorb the beauty
and healing Tera offers us
in each NOW moment.

Photo by Pam Taylor

The Holy Grail II/2/Too[23]

The Holy Grail, the chalice
of my precious human body . . .
is porous.

Each jewel
studding the goblet
is another piece of
energy, love, and work
DONE.

The chalice is porous.
Each jewel now dedicated
to the release of the old liquid,
of that definition of Lizette.

The goblet empties of liquid,
leaving space for light and love.
Not of love given by another,
but of love discovered
and allowed
for Self.

The Holy Grail, the chalice,
then becomes the emptiness,
the nothingness, the ordinariness
that allows it to overflow
with the light of joy
and love for all.

Photo by Pam Taylor

Illusion[24]

One of the dark's
greatest tools
is ILLUSION.

That my mission
is to save,
fix or change
others is
ILLUSION.

My mission
is to walk
the most light
my spirit can radiate.
That is
MY TRUTH.

Rumi Inspired

"We are the pain
and what cures pain.
We are the sweet cold water
and the jar that pours."————Rumi

"We are the pain"
of fixed ideas,
of knowing answers
that don't serve us.

And we cure the pain
through allowing
that gate opening
into a larger garden,
a larger frame,
which asks only for
balance in this moment.
It is neither right nor wrong.
Neither end of the seesaw
being the "correct" way,
but a balance between two truths.

"We are the sweet cold water"
ever fluid, ever searching,
initially for the "right" answer,
then for "the" truth.
And finally we seek the balance
of loving acceptance.
Recognizing that every truth is a lie
at another dimensional frequency.

And we are the "jar that pours."
It is our thoughts,
our intentions that give form
to our lives, our very existence.
The great gift of consciousness
allows us to form
the shape and substance of our jar.
A jar that pours the water
of our "truth" of being
out into the world.

Does your jar pour
"sweet cold water"?

Photo by Pam Taylor

Water and E-Motion

As water represents our emotions,
so can they flare to blind steam,
burning body parts.

Or freeze to solid smooth
unmoving, shiny surfaces
with no give or take.

Our emotions may fall
as gently as snow flakes
piling upon stumps and branches
until their own weight
causes movement:
a branch breaks,
a snow tower topples over.

But hopefully
our emotions flow daily
with such consistent perseverance
as to cut a route through rock.

Hopefully our e-motion
habits cut a path
through the darkness
of old pains and patterns
to new ground.

And in new planes
there is dancing
in the moonlight
of joy.

Moving Center[25]

I move my center
from my head,
from the shoulds,
the gottas,
the ought tos

to - the ripples flowing out
to - the flow of:
I want this,
this feels great.

I move my head
from the driver's seat
to the back seat.

My heart is steering,
life in the fun flow,
a joyride.

In the back seat,
my head's job
is to explain
why we went
where we went,
not determine it.

I move my center
from the poor me
to the power me.

No one else can make **me** happy.
Only I can "save me."

And
I can't make anyone else
truly happy.
Only they can do that.

It's not my job to save anyone.
It's my job to move to my center.
It's my job to move to joy.

Photo by Pam Taylor

The Rat/Horse Race[26]

The horse race is over.
The 10,000 lifetimes of
pounding hooves,
bunched muscles and
billowing breath
with blinders focusing all on
fame, possessions and status
is over.

The race is over.
Blinders removed.
Suddenly a whole field opens.
Our world is widened immeasurably.
Yet for what?

Blinders off,
a whole world is transparent
with choices as open
as the entire field, the sky.

Do you continue to run all out,
circling the open field?
It's the known action.
Is it freedom or lostness,
racing in different directions
without blinders?
What is the destination?

Or do you race
to join the herd,
following the lead mare,
defined by the herd?

Or do you kick out,
blaming others
for the sudden
"loss" of destination?

Or do you drop your
hard-headed history
of knowing with your mind,
into knowing with your heart?

Do you allow your heart-steering
to move you to the center of the field,
or to a small group,
or alone under the shade tree
by trickling water?

Do you allow yourself
to do what heals you,
to pull in the clover-scented fresh air,
the sparking sun, the joy in life?

Do you allow yourself
joy in having a physical life,
of hooves planted on the earth,
in love and joy and gratitude?

Do you allow
your heart-steering
to guide your mission,
to define the new "race"?

Heart Consciousness

I drop my consciousness
from my head
down into my heart.

The head space
is so restricted,
so set in the old patterns
of I want to be "seen"
and accepted by others.

The heart space is so huge
that a thought,
large in "head land"
is a mere dot,
shrunk in the
vast space of the heart.

With the drop into my heart,
I can feel the oddness
of having body parts,
my head and shoulders,
above my consciousness
instead of the free space
so needed above my head.

As I "drop"
into the heart space
it ripples out
and out, and out,
forming concentric circles,
humming and vibrating,
inhabiting a huge space.

Each ripple,
also an orbit
of another merged self,
of self-acceptance,
of self-forgiveness,
of unconditional love
of self.

Photo by Pam Taylor

Light into Dark[27]

The mission,
so simple (!!!)
is to bring
light into the dark.

To bring the light body,
the "body" of my soul,
into my physical body.

The mission is
to unite,
bringing unity to the
body and the soul.

So drop that mental
down the elevator shaft
to the heart
and invite
your light body,
invite your soul
IN.

Photo by Pam Taylor

Silvery Moon of Etznab[28]

The harvest
full moon is
pouring through
the window.
It drenches my heart
in the silver light
of Etznab.

I drop my consciousness
from my head to my heart,
to my root, twelfth
and sacral chakras.
I drop it down to the
life force, transformation
and forgiveness.

I sit in gratitude
for all that is.

Reflected by
the harvest
of her silvery body.

The Sweetness of Doing Nothing[29]

There is such sweetness
in sitting, doing nothing,
allowing my internal reality
to unpack itself.

To lay out on the trading blanket
this and that:
walking on the sand with my sisters,
circling Sedona's Bellrock at sunset,
walking Tyler, wearing a fox-fur hat.
Love shared,
love received.

In the sweetness
of doing nothing,
the mind chatters
until it winds down
and drops into the heart.

Space opens.
Energy moves out
in all directions.
It breathes in.
It breathes out.
"It" is the light.

Within the breathing in and out
is the light running
through the prana tube
of our essence.
The pillar that makes us the
connection between heaven and earth.

Prana or light energy
flows up from Tera
and down from the heavens,
meeting in our heart
then radiating out!

There is such sweetness
in doing nothing.

Photo by Pam Taylor

For Peace[30]

Yang is head
Yin is heart

Yang is mental
Yin is e-motion

Yang needs not
   step down
Yet Yin does need
   to step up

Heart in the driver's seat
mind is the motor

The motor
makes us go
but the heart
steers us aright

Photo by Pam Taylor

Creation Myth

Our creation myth
is to bring light
out of the darkness.

What a perfect palate
of darkness we've created
of murder and mayhem,
starvation and sickness.

Into which we bring
the lightness
of our love and joy,
of our compassion and respect.

Into which we bring
the lightness of
our peace and gratitude.

Into which
we work to keep our focus
on the reality of our life,
on the beauty
of our light
and our world.

Focusing not on the darkness,
but on the light,
on love and peace.

"Inherit the Wind"
by Star York
Photo by Pam Taylor

Hell

How odd
that we would envision
hell inside the Earth,
underground.

When in my truth
it is our not grounding
into our hearts,
that connects us to Tera
that allows for evil—
"live" spelled backwards.

Evil is live turned around,
buried in the dark,
separated from love.

Season's Colors[31]

Vibrant gold
shines from the aspen,
devil's club and willows,
preparing for the
official arrival of fall
next Wednesday.

Yellow gold, in one tradition,
the color of the third chakra,
our power, the seat of our ego.

Tera, dressing for fall in Alaska
also wears cranberry red
close to the ground.
The color of our root chakra:
for safety and survival.

Winter,
the dark hours lengthen,
blackened bare trees
followed with relief
by the white of a pristinely
snow-covered world.

Spring bursts green,
sap and energy moving up.
Green, the color of the heart chakra,
of young love and June weddings.
Green protecting the soft pink
of the underlying heart core.

Tera moves majestically
into the flowering of
the blues, purples and indigos
of the throat, third eye and crown chakra
of the long light of deep summer.

Energy rising through us humans,
the sun's love raining down.
We are each a pillar
connecting heaven and earth.

Photo by Todd Rector

Photo by Pam Taylor

The Woodpecker[32]

The woodpecker
flits from tree to tree,
her bright red crown
seeking the best drum
for her pecking rhythm,
for her call and response
with Tera.

Her red head
pounds a rhythm,
seeking Terra's response,
a mother's heartbeat.

Call and response.

We too beat a rhythm
with our lives.
Are we hearing
Tera's response?

Photo by Todd Rector

Faith

Faith is an artesian well,
ever bubbling up,
ever flowing.

In the dark stillness,
it softens the ground,
feeds the seeds,
glows in reflected
moonlight.

Faith, in the dark,
knows the light will come
however long the balance.

At its best, faith seeps
ever forward,
more ground quickened,
more ground fertile,
more ground reflecting
the light.

Photo by Pam Taylor

Faith 2

Faith is a leap
  into the arms of the Beloved.

Faith is a gift,
  always unwrapped,
    always under the tree.

Faith is knowing the Beloved
  is behind and within
    the darkness
      the pain
        the lostness.

Faith is free.
  Faith is freedom.

Photo by Pam Taylor

2012

To

Oneness

Tea Lights[33]

I lit the tea light
and watched the flame
struggle to climb
down the wick
to the paraffin.

I watched the flame
get smaller and tighter,
leaving burned
blackened wick behind.

A drop of flame
reached the candle body,
and slowly
created a small
pool of melted wax.

Only then did the flame
grow and expand
to include
the entire wick.

So like how we
return to Source.

Pulling in our flame
from the activities
and demands of
day-to-day life.

To burn down
deep within.

Seeking that
large reservoir,
shrinking
our self first.

Reaching down,
with great courage
and faith
as the flame shrinks.
Then finding
Source.

At first hardened,
opaque with our fears,
our old patterns
of what Source
should be.

But as we stay focused,
attention on the small flame,
looking inward,
the surface of true Self
softens,
becomes clear and
turns into fuel
for the larger flame
that is our true Self.
To burn loudly
and large
as One with Source.

Photo by Todd Rector

Water Element

Water is the one element
out of the four:
air, fire, earth and water
that walks in the moccasins
of each of its siblings.

Water floats in the air,
a glittering rainbow
of powdered snow,
drifting weightless
on air currents,
winking at the sun.

When torched by fire it steams mightily,
driving monstrous locomotives
or cleansing human forms
in sightless, yet light-filled,
sweat lodges and steam rooms.

Emulating its sister earth,
water forms itself to the ground.
Huge glaciers bulldoze the earth.
Or ice may cover the earth's surface,
however uneven with smooth and shine.

In its natural state
water flows to contour,
to whatever shape it's given,
from riverbanks to ocean shores.
Always giving in graciously,
uniting and combining
into ONENESS.

Photo by Todd Rector

110

Little Bo Peep
aka Mother Mary

HAS LOST HER SHEEP
    so many of us
    humans
    wandering
    the dry desert

AND DOESN'T KNOW WHERE TO FIND THEM
    they're lost
    in the vast darkness
    of fear and
    fixed patterns

BUT LEAVE THEM ALONE
    we are each
    masters of our lives
    traveling home
    in our own way

AND THEY'LL COME HOME
    all paths
    lead home
    . . . eventually

WAGGING THEIR TAILS BEHIND THEM
    leaving behind
    the duality of
    heaven or hell
    to join in
    ONENESS
    with the Creator

Photo by Todd Rector

God Didn't Call

God never called me.

God is.

God waited

until I noticed

that She is me.

Photo by Pam Taylor

144,000 What?[34]

Are there 144,000
bodies on earth
coded for liftoff in the rapture?
Or
are there 144,000 clans?

My favorite version
from you, Orpheus Phylos,
is that each of us has
144,000 dimensional
aspects of self.

Ascension is the combining
of those aspects.
Merging one into the next.

Another version
of our ancestors,
In Lak'ech.
"I am another yourself."

Photo by Pam Taylor

116

All Along

We ask the light to come in.
We ask Source from out there
to come to us.

When all the time
Source has been here,
deep within us.

Finding Source is simply
a matter of unwrapping
the veils we've used
to protect ourselves.

It is a matter of
identifying the fears and patterns,
the pretensions and defenses.

As the veils unwrap
it becomes clear
that we were hiding Source
from ourselves.

As the veils unwrap,
the wings unfold
the heart soars and
the mind calms.

Source was
there within
all along.

Photo by Pam Taylor

All Ninety-Degree Angles

How is it that
we create all right angles?

Ninty-degree angles in
square picture frames,
reflected in the rectangular
sliding glass doors,
square tiles
and fireplaces.

We nailed Christ to
a cross with ninty-degree angles.

But nature is organic.
Hardly a corner
to be found,
all rounded
softened angles.

We want a God of right angles,
of right and wrong,
of black or white.

Yet life is organic,
full of grays.

Life is not about
what is wrong or right,
but what do you love?
What stirs your passions?
What stirs your heart?

Photo by Todd Rector

120

Breathing God[35]

The eye by which
I see God,
is the eye by which
God sees me.

The breath that
I breathe,
inhaling and exhaling,
is God breathing me.

Abed

The gray silence
is only broken
by the furnace blower.

I lie in the richest purple cocoon
of body warmth under
six inches of down.

The balcony door open,
white-hot cold
filling the room:
a freezer.

My sweet log cabin,
a scaffolding
of blue protection
filled with prayers
and daily meditations.

The warm purple cocoon
in the white cold room
in the blue house.

Home a scaffolding
of blue protection,
filled with prayers.
May the lessons be gentle
and the joy be great.
Full of my listening
rainbow meditations
welcoming in the love

that is neither given nor taken,
but discovered and allowed.

The deep red love
seen and felt
with the eye
through which
I see Creator.
The same eye
through which Creator
sees me.

What joy
and comfort.

Photo by Pam Taylor

Ben: The Missing Link

Today I bridge
heaven with earth:
KA and EL.
As above, so below.

Today is Ben
in the Mayan calendar,
the sky walker.

Today I am the sugarcane,
the stalk growing tall
out of the ground
toward the sun,
bridging heaven and earth.

Indeed
I am the missing link
between heaven and Earth.

Photo by Pam Taylor

126

Creation (My Unit) [36]

The circle of the Godhead
formed a triangle,
ever pointing toward me.

From the triangle in the circle
came the seven flames of spirit,
androgynous
Central Creator.

The seven flames birthed the
twelve eternals,
male and female
seeding genetics to form.

I sit,
the tiniest spark,
yet connected through merges
back to the blue light
of the Godhead.

Photo by Todd Rector

I Breathe Creator's Breath[37]

I breathe Creator's breath in.
I fill with light.
I feel full.
I expand.
My body expands.

I breathe Creator's breath out.
I see the creation of my life.
I see the things,
the blender for my smoothie,
my mephisto sandals I love,
the black shirt I'll wear today.

I breathe Creator's breath in.
All returns to the Oneness.
All becomes the light.
The incredible lightness of being.

I AM
the breath of Creator.
Creator breathes only
as I breathe,
as you breathe,
as we breathe.

We are ONE.

Photo by Pam Taylor

Feather[38]

Today I find
the feather
I AM.

Exploded from
the pillow
of the Beloved.

I drift
so gently,
so effortlessly.

I drift
against
pain and cruelty.

I kiss it.

I drift onto
the bosom
of the Beloved.

I rest.

Photo by Todd Rector

Through Our Eyes

Creator
is the wind
under our wings.

Creator
doesn't tell us
where to fly.

Creator just
allows the wind
we can choose to use
under our wings.

Then Creator
enjoys the new sights
through our eyes.

Snow as the Creator

Snow falling today
and yesterday
and the day before.

Here lies Creator
in solid form.

Each flake
added to the next
until the tree
looks as one.

Oneness.

Covered in Fur

Covered in fur
or feathers,
shells or scales
or skin.

Yet we are
one aspect of the
Great Beloved.

Solstice 2010[39]

I sit in my little pup tent
in the tiny folding chair
in one of these small physical bodies,
with a huge thirty-five-pound crystal,
Our Lady, in my lap.

We are holding space
for the solstice ceremony.

The Kamura clan, my clan,
is drumming,
lined up to the left.

The Aganea clan in full force,
chanting their name,
line the right.

Tera enters,
garbed for initiation
in Her flowing gown
decorated with symbols.

She walks down the aisle
between the two clans,
an unescorted wedding march
to the light.

The ceremony
paves a highway,
builds an access,
across the void
to the dimensions beyond.

Tera allows another layer
of Her onion-skin quarantine
to peel off, to fade away.

Tera welcomes the intense light
from across the void
to bathe and enfold Her.
To permeate Her.

Tera shivers,
cleansing again speeded up,
increased healing here and now.
She soars on the updraft.

Now is the time
for each of us to join Her.
To turn inward
to clear yet another layer
of our onion peel,
another shadow place
seen, loved and forgiven.

We are One.

Photo by Todd Rector

Spring Unfolding

In one week,
last Wednesday to this,
the back drop of the sky
has gone from an X-ray table,
highlighting skeletal trees,
to tiny lace openings
between leaves as they bud-open-flower.

The miracle seems greater
every year that my
precious human body
observes it.

The color has gone
from flat brown
to vibrant minty-mouthwash
tender green.

Each standing person (tree),
inhabiting their whole space,
proudly defining their full belly,
a circle or oval.

Similar to our souls
reaching out to fill in the
bare branches of
our wounded selves
that can't accept
the fresh mint of love.
Or can't allow
the unfolding of new growth.

Our souls work so continuously
to remind our minds
to remind our consciousness
to bud and birth the million leaves of
our joy
our deservedness
our worth.

May you hear and heed your soul.
May you unfold into the fullness
of the truth of ALL that you are
in this spring of our ascension
into the summer of 2012.

Photo by Todd Rector

Life

Our life starts,
carried in the
arms of another.

Later
we leave the family's arms
for comrades in arms:
peers.

Then searching
for a soul mate,
as if another
could make you whole.

And finally
turning both
within and without.
Seeking greater answers.

Discovering yourself finally
alone in the boat,
only to realize that
Source is rowing,
if your free will
allows it so.

All that is asked
of you then
is to listen and
follow guidance.

But one day
the boat bumps
to shore.

And Source, still love and
the wind under your wings,
stops rowing.

And begins asking
over and over again,
what do you want?
What brings you joy?

Oh, you don't like that?
Withdraw your energy.
What would you like?

Co-creators we are.
Creating our life,
living a reality
framed by our perceptions.

No Photon of Darkness[40]

I was taught
there is no evil,
only ignorance.

I struggled.
But what about
cruelty
hatred
torture?

I came to know
that evil is live
spelled backwards,
ignorance in practice.

The physical analogy is:
there is no
particle of darkness.
There are only
particles of light: photons.

Evil, the dark,
has no substance,
no particle of matter,
only an absence of light,
an absence of love.

You can't turn on
the dark.
You can only
deny the light.

Once you shutter yourself,
shield yourself from the light,
as undeserving,
your seemingly "real" world
is but Jung's shadows against
the cave wall,
projected by the fire light,
with no substance
except your belief.

From the high view
evil (dark) is simply
good (light) that
hasn't arrived yet.

I am loving
watching the "light"
arrive in my life.

How is yours?

Endnotes

1. "2012: The End?" - John Major Jenkins has spent his entire career studying Mayan cosmology and its meaning. He is one of the three most prolific and well-known researchers on the Mayan calendar. Jose Arguelles and Carl Johan Calleman are the other two. John Major Jenkins' article, "The Origins of the 2012 Revelation," is in *The Mystery of 2012*. He discusses the fact that the 2012 December solstice sun will align with, or point to, the galactic center of our Milky Way for the first time in 26,000 years. He likens that solstice sun to the hour hand of our earth's processional clock. When it comes around to touch the galactic center, as it will in 2012, our galactic midnight will occur. And that midnight hour can be seen as the beginning of a new day and movement once again toward union with the source. "Time in this conception moves in and out of union with the source. End-date 2012 is not the end of circular time, but the center of time's breathing in and out." p. 65

2. "2012 Creator's Breath" - Claire Montanaro was the first person I read who presented the idea that 2012 is related to the in-breath of Creator. She spoke of Creator breathing in and out on geological time. On the out-breath humanity travels away from Source, away from the light into the darkness, using our free will to create whatever we choose. 2012 represents the in-breath of Creator. The Earth and the galaxy will now be moving back toward Source, towards the light. For more of her information, see her website at: http://www.inluminoglobal.co.uk.

John Major Jenkins presents the same idea in his article, quoted in endnote 1. He both illustrates and speaks to 2012 being the "still point of the out-breath" and identifies the center point as the light of Creator and that we are now at the farthest point away from the center, experiencing our greatest alienation from Source and at the pinnacle of materialism. Now as we hit the midnight of the old era, we then begin moving once again toward the light, towards union with the Creator or Source.

3. "2012 and James Bond" - Arjuna Ardagh has written several books on his research and investigation into modern personal awakenings. He has interviewed hundreds of people concerning their breaking

out of the "trance of separation." He has chosen the title "translucents" for those people who have had radical awakenings. He details those experiences in his book *The Translucent Revolution*. He also has an article in *The Mystery of 2012* titled "The Clock is Ticking." In the article he says, "Sociologists and visionaries like Paul Ray, Barbara Marx Hubbard and Duane Elgin estimate that the number of people whose lives have been touched deeply enough by an awakening to have had a lasting transformative effect to be in the millions, and this number is increasing exponentially. By the early part of the next decade, it could reach 60 to 70 million, or one percent of the world's population." p. 237

In this same article he compares our planetary situation to a James Bond movie with James Bond representing the translucents hard at work in our current world. p. 235

4.   "The Chalice and the Blade" - This poem was inspired by an article channeled by the guardians through Saga-Oracle titled "What Can We Do Together?" in the December 2010 *Sedona Journal*. They write that for eons a "fear-based structure has kept souls in line rather than united in love." The article states that now we are "at the peak of the pyramid of the third-dimensional time node and about to enter the inverted pyramid as you move into the fifth dimension in 2012. The two pyramids joined look like an hourglass, the third (dimension) is the in the blade position, peak up, and the fifth (dimension) in the grail position, peak down. Together they symbolize the Holy Grail, the masculine and feminine in perfect balance . . ." Other symbols for this divine balance are the yin-yang symbol. p. 112

5.   "The Great Will" - This poem was written in 2004 and inspired by my good friend Bev Knox, who asked one day if I believed that God was within me, did I think I was God? It was the perfect question and facilitated the outpouring of this poem, clarifying my life's work on will alignment with the Creator up to that point.

6.   "Made to be Unfolded, Not Molded" - This poem is dedicated to my amazing friend Charlie Johansen-Adams. As the Executive Director of Chugiak Children Services, she had the quote "Children are made to unfolded, they are not made to be molded" painted on the side of one of the Chugiak Children Services Head Start buildings. This quote has been an inspiration for me both as the mother of three children

and as an early interventionist working closely with families and their infants and toddlers. One morning it struck me how this applies not only to our children but to our own spiritual selves and our friends and co-workers.

7.   "The Paradox" - *The Mayan Oracle* talks about the Mayan calendar as a galactic code to the workings of the universe. Within the Tzolkin calendar (one of several Mayan calendars) the individual day in each twenty-day period (similar to our month) is aligned with its own day sign or glyph. These day signs or glyphs repeat themselves in the same order. Each glyph is symbolic of different energies activating awareness of self/cosmos and can be considered a distinct aspect or face of the Creator.

The twelfth Mayan day sign is Eb, which *The Mayan Oracle* defines as "the grail, the golden fleece, the philosopher's stone, the alchemical transmutation that turns baser materials into gold. It is the cornucopia, the paradox of emptiness and harvest, the still place that lies open and fallow, receiving the gifts." In meditating on the paradox of the emptiness combined with the harvest, I thought of the famous story of the master overflowing the tea cup of a supplicant to show him that his mind was already full and unable to accept the "harvest" of new ideas. That brought home to me how we must "empty" our cornucopia's in order to see our true light, the love of Creator from within.

8.   "You Choose" - In the November 2009 *Sedona Journal,* Heather Fraser's article, "The Answer," contained the following: "To ask the divine for the right answer or right thing to do is to clearly deny our power as masterful creators . . . If the divine were to speak to such a request, I'd imagine it would say something like this, 'I have no answer to give you. I am your humble servant. Whatever pain or joy you hold within your heart, whatever lack or abundance you dwell upon in your mind, this is what I will bring to you. I know nothing else but to move in the direction of what you feel. It is your energy of thought and feeling that awakens me into service to you. As your humble servant, I am loyal to whatever energy your thoughts and feelings are requesting. I am not here to give you answers. I am here to simply give. I am here to fill your orders. I am incapable of judgment. I know no right or wrong,

good or bad. I only know how to give. I am the silent nothingness that only moves to create upon your request.' " p. 87

Her words were so exactly how I see the Creator that it inspired me to write "You Choose." You can see more of her work at her website: www.heatherfraser.com.

9. "Groundhog Day" - Imbolic is the ancient holy day celebrating mid-winter, half way between winter solstice and spring equinox. In the old traditions it represents celebration and prophecy, purification and initiation. One way we celebrate mid-winter in America is with Groundhog Day. The movie *Groundhog Day,* staring Bill Murray and Andie McDowell, is one of my all-time favorites. I saw it when I was struggling deeply with whether we, as humans, were evolving or simply stuttering over the same issues of power and greed. In this movie Bill Murray wakes up to the same day over and over. With humor and emotional depth, we watch him act out human development from stage one to stage three that Ken Wilber talks about in *Kosmic Consciousness.* In stage one the Bill Murray character cares only for himself: robbing banks, stealing the groundhog and trying to commit suicide. As the days continue to repeat themselves he moves to stage two, caring for others in his small group. He falls for Andie McDowell, but she accurately reads his courting as manipulations to get her into his bed. Eventually he moves to stage three of universal caring. In the final stages of the movie he has chosen the joy found in serving the community from catching the boy falling out of the tree to the saving of the older man choking on a bite of steak. At that point Andie McDowell sees him as trustworthy and chooses him. His reward is both her caring and the days once again proceeding. I watch this movie each Groundhog Day and celebrate our human evolution.

10. "Shift Happens" - Todd Rector is not only an excellent photographer, as evidenced by many of the photos in this book, but a powerful healer and good friend. Some of my favorite poems ("Shift Happens" and "Deliver Us") have come to me whole while driving home from a session with him through the beautiful Matanuska Valley. This poem was written the day after Thanksgiving, recognizing the shifts happening in my life.

150

11. "The Path" - Hope, Alaska, is a small community across Turnagain Arm from Anchorage. Old mining roads reach up into the mountains behind the town. One mountainside has an extended stand of aspen trees that turn gold in the fall. I travel there each September for my birthday. In Coeur D'Alene, a tiny informal campground I've been visiting for decades, I found the old familiar trail going up the creek completely blocked. Spruce beetle kill combined with high winds had knocked down the huge old trees that had once lined the path. Now there was brilliant sunshine, where once all had been shadowed, and the trail was crosshatched with gigantic trunks lying like a giant game of pick-up sticks making the trail completely impassable. All this new light, yet the old path was gone. The experience was such a metaphor for my inner life.

12. "Deliver Us" - This poem was written on the drive home from another session with Todd Rector, photographer and friend. I was driving through the majestic Matanuska Valley, listening to the sound track from *The Prince of Egypt*, the biblical story of Moses. I was singing along with "Deliver Us," in which the Jews are asking God to deliver them from slavery under the Egyptian pharaoh, when I suddenly had a flash of how much of my earlier life I'd spent asking for someone to deliver me. How much of my life I'd spent asking for someone to release me from my self-imposed slavery. In my younger years I thought it was a man who would somehow deliver me. Then it was Christ or a teacher who was to deliver me. Asking for spiritual deliverance reminded me of the wonderful line Hoyt Axton sings in "Life Machine" that "everyone wants a ride to heaven but nobody wants to make the climb." So many people want someone to come along to give them a free spiritual ride. They don't want to have to do the daily work or climb that is necessary to get to heaven in my reality.

And that, wanting so much for someone else, a greater spiritual leader, to come give you a ride to heaven took me to one of my favorite quotes in *ET 101* telling us that now is "no longer the time of great spiritual teachers. It is now the time of great spirits instead." For me, that quote is such a great reminder that we each have to deliver ourselves. We can't count on Christ to return to carry us, or any great spiritual leader to give us a ride up to heaven. We have to make the climb and deliver ourselves. p. 62

13. "I scrub the Pot 2"- I love the image of our soul as a pot filled with the "water" of the light and love of our essence Creator. The water, our original face, comes in clean and clear. As we have experimented with this free-will zone, our souls have accumulated residue in the pot. We can choose to leave the residue alone, pretending it's not there, but it creates a filter of pain or judgment through which we then see the world. Or we can scrub away at those old wounds, cleaning the pot, processing our pain. And that dirties the water. It is as if we were to take a burned pot off the stove. When we first pour in clean water it remains clear until we start scrubbing, then the pot gets cleaner, and the water gets dirtier. But the dirty water can be simply poured out and the pot remains cleaner. I wrote this poem sitting in the hospital with my amazing friend, Charlie Johansen-Adams, who had just had surgery to remove some of her pot's residue.

14. "The Mission" – My beautiful-hearted friend, Pam Walling, invited me to a long weekend at the Ventana Resort in Arizona. We hiked and processed and shared deeply. And what clarified for me in our discussions was how important it is that our mission focus on walking, standing and flowing absolutely as much light as we can. And how easily I have gotten side-tracked in focusing on how much light someone else could or should be walking.

15. "I Have No Authority Figure" – *The Kosmic Consciousness* audio tapes by Ken Wilber are so powerful. His clear articulation of being one with "all that arises" so confirmed and fueled my first-hand experiences of seeing the light within.

16. "Marrying Your Dark Side" - In the September 2009 *Sedona Journal*, in her article "Tools for Transformation: What If?" Daniele DeVoe wrote: "What if you loved yourself—just for today? Self-judgment is one of the most difficult problems rampant in your world today . . . If you truly loved yourself, would you live one more moment in your present circumstances? Would you work to change or improve your life? Would you share that love with people in your life? A few more 'what ifs' to ponder: What if I saw myself through the eyes and heart of my own sacred soul and simply loved everything I saw? What if I loved my personality – my ego, the original, individuating gift given to

152

me by Source – rather than treating it like a sad, negative, unwanted mistake?" p. 13

17. "E-Motion" - An article entitled "Forgiveness . . . With a Twist" was written by Ruth Evelyn in the *Sedona Journal*, June 2010. She wrote, "We all experience the same emotions. Emotions are frequencies of energy vibrating at various rates of motion. Emotions are energy in motion – e-motion. When you look at anything you desire to improve in your life, look no further than the emotional field in your body before you consider changing the behavior of another or our outside circumstance. Your emotional body is the palette of paints with which you are coloring your life. If you do not change the palette, you will create the same landscape elsewhere." p. 89

One of my favorite sayings is "Wherever you go, there you are." It is the same idea.

18. "The Road Less Traveled" - This poem flowed out of me after thinking that three different friends were upset with me as I stood in my truth or said no, setting boundaries in place. Yet when I asked them, no one was upset. It was all my projection. It reminded me of *ET101's* version of emotional body surgery. They say "This surgical procedure requires conscious participation and cannot be done under anesthetic. In fact, many of you will have to come out of the anesthetics you are currently under in order to participate . . . traveling over darkened and repulsive terrain . . . because there is no way around this one. Lightness and darkness cannot coexist in the same place at the same time . . . The fact is, the only thing more painful than going through this procedure is not going through it." p. 75

19. "The Roadrunner" - My closest friend and spiritual sister, Len Whitebear, and I have completed over 118 channelings with information initially coming from Vega, and eventually from sources across the void. That information is embedded deeply in my being and in the outpouring of poetry. I spent a month with her in January of 2009 and loved the Arizona landscape and animals and birds. Have you ever seen a roadrunner and the funny position they assume as they hustle across the desert?

20. "Working in Our Sleep" - This poem was inspired from drawing the "Greed/Beyond Greed" card in the OSHO *Transformation Tarot*. Osho's story to explain greed is about the ancient sage working hard at enlightenment for many years and lifetimes. He asks the saint Narada, who serves as a postman between paradise and earth, to ask how long until he's enlightened. A young man nearby, dancing and playing music, is uninterested in that question. In paradise Narada asks for enlightenment timelines for both. When he brings the information back, the answer of three more lifetimes infuriates the sage. In contrast the young man celebrates, "Just as many leaves as are on this tree? That is not very far, then I have already arrived!—just think how many trees there are on the whole earth. Compared! So it is very close. Thank you, sire, that you inquired." And in that moment he was enlightened. It is in humor, play, and joy that we en-light-ten. More information is available at http://www.osho.com/ p. 23

21. "In-Form-Mation" - is simply another version of my reality, which has been deeply impacted since the early '90s by the quote below from *ET 101*. The book states that there are as many realities as there are people alive to create them. And that global reality is merely a group consensus on a few minor points. "The reality that you live is nothing more than an audio-visual demonstration of where your attention is." p. 19

22. "Praying Mantis" - This poem is dedicated to Caroline Voors, a fantastic traveling companion and friend. Her gift to me of *Animal-Speak Runes* by Ted Andrews inspired this poem. I drew the praying mantis rune one morning. With this rune Andrews recommends time to "still the mind and body in order to grasp new insight and new nourishment within your life." He recommends the use of stillness and camouflage for both protection and to go within to draw upon the greater power through meditation, contemplation or dreams. p. 88

23. "The Holy Grail II/2/ Too" - Two of the primary concepts in this poem come from *The Mayan Oracle*. Eb is the twelfth day sign or glyph in the Mayan calendar's twenty-day cycle. The affirmation for Eb is "I am an open chalice. I am the joyful expression of the abundance of the universe." Seeing our bodies as a chalice, as one version of the Holy Grail, inspired a number of poems for me. p. 90

154

The Mayan Oracle is also the source of the profound awareness on my part of the truth of "Love just is, and because love is neither given nor taken, but rather discovered and allowed, you are a natural part of the circulation of its energy." In this thought I recognized the truth that it does not matter how much love I give someone else, but rather how much love they can allow themselves to receive. And conversely, how much love I can receive from another is directly related to how much I think I deserve to receive. This has profoundly impacted my relationships. p. 47

24. "Illusion" - A long hike into Ventana Canyon and deep conversation with my good friend, Pam Walling, again reminded me of my mission to walk my light, not save another. *ET 101* labels our desire to save others the dreaded messiah complex, and identifies it as the most important pitfall we fall into as we awaken. They clarify that the true mission is not about 'saving' anyone. They look at each person on the planet as a master knowing the game and having a right to their own decision, including continuing as a master of limitation. "Saving people from their rights is not the intention of this planetary mission." And running around saving folks from their own free will is not part of the mission. We each must be the choice we have made. p. 57-58

25. "Moving Center" - On the first day of each month Lena Stevens posts an update for the following month on her website http://www.thepowerpath.com/. My poem, "Moving Center," was inspired by her January 2010 posting which was titled "Moving Center." In it she wrote, "We are now fully engaged in this year's (2010) moving centered time. This is not the month for 'too much thinking.' . . . Think of this time as a re-training of your mind. It is no longer in the primary decision maker's position but rather in the back seat as a good tool that can help you define your reality in hindsight. Rely on your gut feelings. When you make the right decision from the gut, you will feel, an instant relief that may not make any rational sense at the time but will certainly come clear in the future."

26. "The Rat/Horse Race" - This poem was inspired by an article channeled by Selacia titled "A Time of Transparency" in the December '09 *Sedona Journal*. She wrote that in 2010 everything would become more transparent as we deeply re-examine what is real. She likened the

process to being a racehorse, with the blinders removed after the race and turned out to pasture. The race horse has so many choices at that point, as do we. p.46

27. "Light Into Dark" - This poem was inspired by Sheldon Niddle's comments in *You Are Becoming a Galactic Human Being*. Virginia Essene asks him to elaborate on his earlier comment about uniting the soul with the physical aspects of material creation. He responds with "The light soul forms the light body. Since it is a physical universe, the light soul or soul force has created a physical aspect of the light body or the physical body. These energies together form a unity of physical body and soul or light body . . . One unites them together to form a path of light that enables the physical universe to evolve to its full potential and also allows the spiritual universe likewise to live through the physical to evolve into what its fully capable of being." p. 133

28. "Silvery Moon of Etznab" - Etznab is the eighteenth Mayan glyph or day sign representing the universal energy or aspect of Creator for that day. I have followed the Mayan calendar since the early 1990s by meditating on the energy of that day's sign or glyph each morning. Some of my most powerful meditations have been with Etznab and the sword initiation suggested in *The Mayan Oracle* of asking the Archangel Michael to use his sword of truth to link our heads directly with our hearts. The color for Etznab is silver. This poem flowed on an Etznab morning. p. 118

29. "The Sweetness of Doing Nothing" - This poem is dedicated to Susan Garner and her friend. They were trying to recall the Italian word for the sweetness of doing nothing that Elizabeth Gilbert talks about in her wonderful book, *Eat, Pray, Love*.

30. "For Peace" - This poem was inspired by Onereon through Jeff Michael's article "Balancing Earth's Energies" in the February 2011 *Sedona Journal*. In his paragraph about the energy of being human, he talks about the mixture of energies each of us carries, sometimes called female and male energies, or yin and yang, which represent peace and action. When human energy is imbalanced the energies become passive and aggressive. He links thought with yang energy and emotions with yin energies. The energy balance on the planet now—and for several centuries past—has been imbalanced male or yang energy that is ag-

gressive. He acknowledges the current movement to raise the female or yin energy of peace. He states that it "is not a lowering of the yang energy that will allow progress. Yang propels progress. It is the raising of yin that brings purpose to the action of such a strong yang energy." p. 67-68

31. "Season's Colors" - I started writing this poem in the fall, September of 2010, and finished editing it May 9, 2011. So the poem clearly has the feel of a present fall going into winter and the spring sap-rising time. This was an anomaly for me, as most of my poems just flow onto paper with little editing. This one sat in the birth canal for over half a year.

32. "The Woodpecker" - Like "Praying Mantis," this poem is dedicated to Caroline Voors, my fantastic traveling companion and friend who gifted me with *Animal-Speak Runes* by Ted Andrews. He ties the woodpecker to new rhythms, and speaks to their drumming on trees linking them to Tera's heartbeat. He then reminds us to follow our own rhythms and work toward goals in our own unique way, not simply replicating past paths, but following the new opportunities for rapid growth available. p. 111

33. "Tea Lights" - My incredibly generous friend, Molly Merritt-Duran, has shared her Trapper Creek cabin freely with me for fifteen years. I have written a number of poems at the cabin. This one came to me, sitting in the outhouse which she has beautifully painted with fireweed, lighting some incense and then a tea light candle.

34. "144,000 What?" - It is quite amazing to look at the many allusions to the significance of the number 144,000. Starting with the biblical 144,000 chosen ones all the way to the 144 crystal grid, about which the Archangel Metatron has channeled information through both Tyberon and David Miller in numerous *Sedona Journal* articles. But my favorite version or translation of 144,000 is in *From Earth, the Cosmos and You*, by Orpheus Phylos and Virginia Essene. They state that we each "have 144,000 dimensional aspects of self, all of which have split off from the soul's beginning nature and are simultaneously evolving through other worlds even now. Somewhere in time, all aspects will find each other and come back into original divineness. Then the soul seed will choose to re-create itself again into a grander degree

of glory that awaits all the souls in their higher consciousness ascension." p. 73

For me ascension is the recombining, or merging of our physical form consciousness with our higher selves. In the early years of my spiritual work I thought of the higher self aspect of myself as my guardian angel or my guide. My meditations led me to begin a merging of my "molecules" into my much larger higher self who appeared as a tall column of silver white energy. I remember how surprised I was, when after almost three years of that combining, to have a round golden ball of light come as we were setting up a teepee for ceremony. Who are you, I wanted to know. I'm already merged with my higher self. And so began the next level of merging in 1992. Since then nine more aspects of myself have come to be merged into one unit.

35. "Breathing God" - Master Djwhal Khul through Kathelyn Kingdon wrote an article, "Assist in the Process of Planetary Purification" in the April 2010 *Sedona Journal*. Her article quoted the thirteenth-century German theologian, Meister Eckhart Von Hochheim, writing "The eye by which I see God is the eye by which God sees me." This quote was profound for me as a way of actually seeing (so to speak) what I believe and have experienced in my relationship with Creator. On one level I believe that it is through my eyes that Creator is able to see the physically manifested world. It is through my eye or my belief structure, that I imagine/create Creator in my image. My God's love matches my self-acceptance of how much love I deserve to receive. From yet another view, believing that Creator/God is within me then the eye is actually the same eye, with Creator having billions of eyes to see through, while I have two. p. 29

36. "Creation (My Unit)" - This poem was inspired by a combination of two different sources. One is information Orpheus Phylos channeled from the Archangel Michael in *Earth, the Cosmos and You* in a chapter titled "The Tribunal Godhead and the Holographic Computer." In it he attempts to give us a visionary image of what he calls the Tribunal Godhead or Divine Circle, the creation of the seven flames of spirit and their birthing of the twelve eternals. It is a fascinating description of creation. p. 71-73.

158

The other inspiration was channeling session 117 between Len Whitebear and me. The sources gave us information on the merging of higher selves we had accomplished on this side of the void and the multiple merges connected from across the void. They titled that combination of merges from both sides of the void as a Unit. And they spoke to the critical importance of putting aside inviolate time for creative endeavors.

37. "I Breathe Creator's Breath" - For many years in my early spiritual work my daily prayers were some version of "God make my eyes thy eyes, make my tongue thy tongue" etc. When I found the following Invocation in Ralph Blum's *The Book of Runes* it replaced my individual prayers and remains one of my favorites.

> God within me, God without,
> How shall I ever be in doubt?
> There is no place where I may go
> And not there see God's face, not know
> I am God's vision and God's ears.
> So through the harvest of my years
> I am the Sower and the Sown,
> God's Self unfolding and God's own.

"I Breathe Creator's Breath" flowed out of a meditation in which this was a visceral experience, no longer a mental request but my deep truth.

38. "The Feather" - Unlike the majority of poems in this book, this is one of just five that were written eight years ago. At that time I was a full-time (meaning working seventy hours a week) Executive Director of a growing non-profit agency, FOCUS, Inc. I meditated each morning, and any weekend hours not at the office were spent on spiritual meditation, initiations, and reading. Oriah Mountain Keeper's book, *The Call*, moved me deeply and inspired the oneness found in this poem.

39. "Solstice 2010" - This poem was what I experienced camping alone on the Liberty Falls River near Chitna, Alaska, on June 21, 2010. Our Lady, the thirty-five-pound crystal whom I have been honored to steward for twenty years, let me know she wanted to travel with me.

This was a very unusual request, as typically she resided in my meditation room, rarely even attending ceremonies. Much of the solstice weekend she sat outside in a camp chair, overlooking the roaring Liberty River. For the ceremony, with a light rain falling, we sat together inside my pup tent. It was a very powerful experience.

40. "No Photon of Darkness" - The idea for this poem was inspired by Virginia Essene's interview with Ernest Fruest in *Energy Blessings From the Stars*. She refers to an earlier quote of his "without the soul the body is lifeless clay; without the body the soul is a flower without earth." Isn't that beautiful?

Then she asks him why we humans aren't living that marriage of flesh and spirit? He responds with an analogy describing people as a lamp whose lens has become encrusted but with pure light in the lamp's interior. The dirty lens represents the imperfections and distortions of the personality. Our job is to clean the glass. He refers to evil as the interference of the personality (dirt) with our pure soul (light). "Evil is simply the absence of good. From a higher perspective, evil is good which hasn't arrived. To use a physical analogy, there is a particle of light, namely a photon, but there is no particle of blackness. If a room is dark, it's not because there's something called a 'black on' being emitted; it's because there's an absence of light." p. 156

REFERENCES

Note: Books marked with an asterisk (*) are those that have had the greatest impact for me and that I highly recommend.

Andrews, Ted. *Animal-Speak Runes*. Jackson, Tennessee: Dragonhawk Publishing, 2009.

Ardagh, Arjuna. *The Translucent Revolution: How People Just Like You are Waking Up and Changing the World*. Norvato, California: New World Library, 2005.

Barks, Coleman with John Moyne, A.J. Arberry and Reynold Nicholson. *The Essential Rumi*. Edison, New Jersey: Castle Books, 1997.

Blum, Ralph. *The Book of Runes: A Handbook for the Use of an Ancient Oracle: The Viking Runes*. New York: St. Martin's Press, 1993.

Braden, Gregg. *Fractal Time: The Secret of 2012 and a New World Age*. Carlsbad, California: Hay House Inc., 2009.

Calleman, Carl Johan. *The Mayan Calendar and the Transformation of Consciousness*. Rochester, Vermont: Bear and Co. Publishing, 2004.

Carey, Ken. *Vision*. Kansas City, Missouri: Uni*Sun, 1985.

Christ, The. *New Teaching for an Awakening Humanity*. Santa Clara, California: Spiritual Education Endeavors Publishing, 1986.

Churchward, Colonel James. *The Sacred Symbols of Mu*. New York: Coronet Communications, 1933.

———. *The Cosmic Forces of Mu*. New York: Coronet Communications, 1934.

———. *The Second Book of the Cosmic Forces of Mu*. New York: Coronet Communications, 1935.

DeRohan, Ceanne. *Original Cause: The Unseen Role of Denial*. Santa Fe, New Mexico: One World Publications, 1986.

Emoto, Masaru. *The Hidden Messages in Water*. Hillsboro, Oregon: Beyond Words Publishing, 2004.

Essene, Virginia and Irving Fruest. *Energy Blessings from the Stars: Seven Initiations*. Santa Clara, California: Spiritual Education Endeavors Publishing, 1998.

Essene, Virginia and Sheldon Nidle. *You Are Becoming a Galactic Human*. Santa Clara, California: Spiritual Education Endeavors Publishing, 1994.*

Gilbert, Elizabeth. *Eat, Pray, Love: One Woman's Search for Everything Across Italy, India, and Indonesia*. New York: Penguin Books, 2007.

Hand Clow, Barbara. *The Mayan Code: Time Acceleration and Awakening the World Mind*. Rochester, Vermont: Bear and Co. Publishing, 2007.

———. *The Pleiadian Agenda: A New Cosmology for the Age of Light*. Rochester, Vermont: Bear and Co. Publishing, 1995.

———. *Catastrophobia: The Truth Behind Earth Changes in the Coming Age of Light*. Rochester, Vermont: Bear and Co. Publishing, 2001.

Hawkins, David R. *Power vs. Force: The Hidden Determinants for Human Behavior*. Carlsbad, California: Hay House Publishers, 2002.*

Hay, Louise L. *You Can Heal Your Life*. Carson, California: Hay House, Inc., 1984.

Katie, Byron with Stephen Mitchell. *A Thousand Names for Joy: Living in Harmony with the Way Things Are*. New York: Crown Publishing Group, 2007.

Kenyon, Tom and Virginia Essene. *The Hathor Material: Messages from an Ascended Civilization*. Santa Clara, California: Spiritual Education Endeavors Publishing, 1998.

Kryon. *The End Times: New Information for Personal Peace*. Del Mar, California: The Kryon Writings, 1992.

Ladinsky, Daniel. *Love Poems from God: Twelve Sacred Voices from the East and West*. New York: Penquin Compass, 2002.*

Lappi, Diana. *ET 101: The Cosmic Instruction Manual: An Emergency Remedial Edition*. Santa Fe, New Mexico: Intergalactic Council Publication, 1990.*

Marciniak, Barbara. *Bringers of the Dawn: Teachings from the Pleiadians*. Santa Fe, New Mexico: Bear and Company Publishing, 1992.

Marciniak, Barbara, Karen Marciniak and Tera Thomas. *Earth Pleiadian Keys for the Living Library*. Santa Fe, New Mexico: Bear and Company Publishing, 1995.

Melchizedek, Drunvalo. *Serpent of Light Beyond 2012: The Movement of the Earth's Kundalini and the Rise of the Female Light 1949 to 2013*. San Francisco: Red Shell/Weiser, 2008.

———. *The Ancient Secret of the Flower of Life*, Vol. 1. Flagstaff, Arizona: Light Technology Publishing, 1998.

Mountain Dreamer, Oriah. *The Call: Discovering Why You Are Here*. New York: HarperCollins Publishers, 2003.

Osho. *Osho Transformation Tarot: Insights and Parables for Renewal in Everyday Life*. New York: St. Martins Press, 1999.

Palmer, Helen. *Enneagram: Understanding Yourself and the Others in Your Life*. San Francisco: HarperSanFrancisco, 1988.

Phylos, Orpheus and Virginia Essene. *Earth, the Cosmos and You: Revelations by Archangel Michael*. Santa Clara, California: Spiritual Education Endeavors Publishing, 1999.

Quan Yin, Amorah. *The Pleiadian Workbook: Awakening Divine Ka*. Rochester, Vermont: Bear and Co. Publishing, 1996.

———. *The Pleiadian Tantric Workbook: Awakening Divine Ba*. Rochester, Vermont: Bear and Co. Publishing, 1997

———. *Affinity: Reclaiming the Divine Flow of Creation*. Rochester, Vermont: Bear and Co. Publishing, 2001.*

Raphael. *The Starseed Transmissions: An Extraterrestrial Report*. Kansas City, Missouri: Uni*Sun, 1982.

Rosenberg, Marshall B. *Nonviolent Communication: A Language of Life*. Encinitas, California: PuddleDancer Press, 2005.

Sams, Jamie. *Medicine Cards: The Discovery of Power Through the Ways of Animals*. Sante Fe, New Mexico: Bear & Company, 1988.

———. *Sacred Path Cards: The Discovery of Self Through Native Teachings*. San Francisco: HarperSanFrancisco, 1990.

Spilsbury, Ariel and Michael Bryner. *The Mayan Oracle: Return Path to the Stars*. Santa Fe, New Mexico: Bear and Co. Publishing, 1992.*

Solara, *The Legend of Altazar: A Fragment of the True History of Planet Earth*. Portal, Arizona: Star-Borne Unlimited, 1987.

————. *Part One of the 11:11 Trilogy: EL*AN*RA, The Healing of Orion*. Charlottesville, Virginia: Star-Borne Unlimited, 1991.*

————.*11:11: Inside the Doorway*. Charlottesville, Virginia: Star-Borne Unlimited, 1992.

Sounds True (edited), *The Mystery of 2012: Predictions, Prophecies and Possibilities*. Boulder, Colorado: Sounds True, 2009.

Valentin, Ann and Virginia Essene. *Cosmic Revelation*. Santa Clara, California: Spiritual Education Endeavors Publishing, 1987.

Wilber, Ken, Terry Patten, Adam Leonard and Marco Morelli. *Intregral Life Practices: A 21st Century Blueprint for Physical Health, Emotional Balance, Mental Clarity and Spiritual Awakening*. Boston: Intregral Books, 2008.

Wilber, Ken. *Kosmic Consciousness*. An audio course. Boulder, Colorado: Sounds True, 2008.*

Wright, Machaelle Small. *MAP: The Co-Creative White Brotherhood Medical Assistance Program*. Warrenton, Virginia: Perelandra, Ltd., 1990.

WEB-BASED SOURCES

http://www.thepowerpath.com
http://www.tomkenyon.com
http://www.spiritofmaat.com
http://www.osho.com
http://www.inluminoglobal.co.uk
For Heather Fraser: http://www.sacredscribe.com

ABOUT THE PHOTOGRAPHER

PAM TAYLOR

Pam Taylor grew up in a United Nations community of New York City. Surrounded by people of different countries, she developed a love of travel and diverse cultures. Her first media job, as a researcher for CBS News documentaries, plunged her into a world of images and words. In the late '70s, as a photojournalist stringer for Associated Press, she covered the civil war in Nicaragua, the Panama Canal treaties, and the Shah of Iran in Panama. Her photos from this period appeared in many publications including *The New York Times, The Washington Post, Time,* and *Newsweek.*

Taylor's career took her to Southeast Asia where she supplied photos to the U.S. Army of medical research projects in Thailand and the People's Republic of China.

Living in Thailand during '60s, Taylor detoured from journalism and began documenting Thai art. Her photographs were featured in magazines and books.

In 1995 Oxford University Press published *Birds, Beasts, and Blossoms in Thai Art* written and illustrated by Pam Taylor.

Her photographs have appeared in numerous books including *Thai Temples and Thai Temples and Murals,* Oxford University Press; *Burma's Revolution of the Spirit,* Aperture Press; and the cover of *Silence,* Innisfree Press. In Peru, Taylor took pictures of local artists whose work depicted the decade-long civil war between government forces and the Shining Path, a guerrilla terrorist group.

Upon returning to the United States, Taylor earned an MA in education from Johns Hopkins University. In 2003 she moved to Arizona to teach English and outdoor skills at a small international boarding school. With a grant from the Arizona Heritage Project, Taylor and her high school students produced a DVD with student digital stories and a documentary about ancient Native American cultures of northern Arizona. The work is archived at the U.S. Library of Congress.

Taylor continues to produce multi-media documentaries. Some of these include stories, interviews, images, and videos about New Mexico artists and their work. At present she is working on documentaries about homeless veterans in Arizona and another on poverty in the central Arizona. She is working with the community of Hannibal, Missouri, to teach teenagers how to produce oral histories about racism.

Her work can be found on:

www.pamtaylorphotography.com

www.pamtaylormultimedia.com

ABOUT THE PHOTOGRAPHER

TODD RECTOR

Todd and Alisa at Chena Hot Springs before the baby

Todd was born in Michigan on June 1, 1972, and shortly thereafter moved to Germany. Over the early part of his life he lived in Vermont, Florida, and Virginia, where he found his deep love for the ocean and the natural world. In doing so he has cultivated a life as a surfer and an avid outdoor enthusiast, surfing and playing in the outdoors both here in Alaska and Outside.

Todd moved to Alaska to attend the University of Alaska at Fairbanks, where he earned a degree in cultural anthropology with a focus on Alaska Native culture and art. It is out of this love for the Native people of Alaska that he cultivated a desire to do Native art. He spent several years studying with Native Aleut artist, Alvin Amason, where he made masks, drums, and various other traditional Native ethnological arts. In 2003 he won an honorable mention for a pair of box turtle rattles he made that year. He continues to carve and paint to the present day, masks being a strong focus.

After graduating he moved to the Anchorage area, pursuing martial arts training that he continues today, training in Tai Chi and various forms of Kung Fu and Qigong. It is out of his love for the internal martial arts that he cultivated a desire and love for the healing arts, pursuing a career as a massage and manual therapist.

Todd got into photography after borrowing his twin sister's camera to take some shots while visiting her four years ago in California. She was so blown away with his natural ability and apparent "photographer's eye" that she saw in the photos, she decided to get him a digital camera for Christmas that year. With that present, Todd has continued to cultivate his photographer's eye to capture "the beauty he sees in the world," as he puts it. He has amassed several thousand photos, some of which you see in this book.

This is the first time he has shared his work publicly, and Lizette is proud to have it be part of her book.

ABOUT THE AUTHOR

LIZETTE ESTELLE STIEHR

Lizette has spent a significant portion of her life consciously dedicated to spiritual growth and service. She began daily meditation in her early thirties, starting with an eleven-year inner mystery correspondence course through BOTA, The Builders of the Adytum. Lizette has followed an eclectic spiritual path such as the Course in Miracles. As an astrologer she has done more than nine hundred life-mission readings. A thirty-five pound crystal, Our Lady, was entrusted to Lizette for stewardship. An e-book, *Divine Inspirations: Stories of Awakening and Empowerment* begins with the story of Our Lady coming to Lizette. It is available through http://www.ourweepingangel.org.

Lizette has initiated and participated in numerous meditation groups and ceremonies. She has been in active contact with her guides since 1980 and actively followed their guidance through life changes, initiations and information downloads. Len Whitebear and Lizette have collaborated on 118 channelings of information concerning humanity, our beloved planet, this solar system, and the galaxy.

Lizette has always held a deep interest in native spirituality. In 1993 she began utilizing the Mayan calendar day sign or glyph as a focal point for meditation. She has also studied the larger cycles of the Mayan calendar, including information on 2012. This dedication and the great clearing it has offered her is reflected in the poems in this book. The endnotes offer more specific information on that linkage.

Her great avocations include outdoor activities, travel, and writing poetry. This book of poetry expresses the deep longing in Lizette's soul for expression in the world. Her poetry has been published in the *Sedona Journal*, in *Alaska Women Speak* and recognized in the semifinal round of the National Amateur Poetry Competition. A blog of her inspirational poetry can be found at Lizette Stiehr.blogspot.com.

Lizette arrived in Alaska in 1974 with a masters degree in special education and has worked professionally in the field of disabilities. She worked as a statewide program manager for the State of Alaska Health & Social Services Early Intervention Program, and later as the Executive Director of FOCUS, Inc., a non-profit agency. She has received numerous professional awards from the field and the many boards on which she's served, including inclusion in Who's Who in American Women in 2005.

As a mother, Lizette thoroughly enjoyed raising her three children and getting to see the world through their very different perceptions. They now bless her with their exquisite parenting of her eight grandchildren who are an active part of her life.

Order Form

I would like to order my own or another copy of the book *2012 to Oneness* by Lizette Estelle Stiehr. Please send me:

books x $22.00 per copy = _____

+ Postage (first class) & handling @ $4.95/book: _____

TOTAL ENCLOSED $ _____

We accept cash, check, or money order made out to Northbooks, or VISA, Mastercard. Prices subject to change without notice.

(You may phone your VISA/MC order to Northbooks at 907-696-8973)

VISA/MC card # ⬜⬜⬜⬜ ⬜⬜⬜⬜ ⬜⬜⬜⬜ ⬜⬜⬜⬜

Exp. date: _____ / _____   Amount charged: $ _____

Signature: _____

Phone number: _____

Please send my book (s) to:

Name: _____

Address: _____

City: _____ State: _____ Zip: _____

Fill out this order form and send to:

NORTHBOOKS
11915 Lazy Street, Ste. C
Eagle River, AK 99577-7898
(907) 696-8973
www.northbooks.com

CPSIA information can be obtained at www.ICGtesting.com
Printed in the USA
LVOW110302160911

246434LV00005B/1/P